# CLASS 68
# AND CLASS 88
# LOCOMOTIVES

## JOHN JACKSON

AMBERLEY

First published 2023

Amberley Publishing
The Hill, Stroud
Gloucestershire, GL5 4EP

www.amberley-books.com

Copyright © John Jackson, 2023

The right of John Jackson to be identified as
the Author of this work has been asserted in
accordance with the Copyrights, Designs and
Patents Act 1988.

ISBN 978 1 4456 8316 4 (print)
ISBN 978 1 4456 8317 1 (ebook)

British Library Cataloguing in Publication Data.
A catalogue record for this book is available from
the British Library.

Origination by Amberley Publishing.
Printed in the UK.

# Contents

# Introduction

The two classes of locomotives featured in this book are both operated by Direct Rail Services (DRS). This company was created in the mid-1990s by British Nuclear Fuels Ltd (BNFL). In its early days, the main business was the movement of nuclear material, which had been handled by British Rail prior to the privatisation of the UK's railways during that decade.

In 2005, the ownership of Direct Rail Services transferred from BNFL to the Nuclear Decommissioning Authority (NDA). By that time the company had diversified into other rail traffic movements, notably operating intermodal freight services, particularly between England and Scotland. In 2021, DRS was placed under the control of Nuclear Transport Solutions (NTS). This company 'specialises in providing solutions to complex nuclear transport and logistics challenges'. In May 2021, the company announced a rebranding of Direct Rail Services with a view to aligning its identity more closely to that of the NTS parent brand. The company claims that, given time, the locos themselves will come to reflect this new branding but, at the time of writing, DRS are still working on the most cost-effective way of achieving this aim.

So, let us take a brief look into DRS's history. At the outset, the company's rail operations were in the hands of veteran English Electric Type 1 Class 20 locomotives, dating back to the late 1950s and early 1960s. Five of these diesel machines were soon joined by a variety of former British Rail classes as the company expanded its loco fleet. These included locos from classes 33, 37, 47 and 57, all of which proved popular among rail enthusiasts anxious to see an extension to the working lives of these elderly machines. Later, in common with other freight operators, DRS also bolstered its fleet with the acquisition of Class 66 locomotives, including five on long-term lease from DB Cargo Ltd.

Operating factors within this diesel fleet, such as their increasing unreliability and the reducing availability of spares, led to the company considering a new approach to its choice of motive power.

It was at the beginning of 2012 that, as one of the UK's major freight operators, DRS announced the placing of an order for the UK's first batch of what was to become the Class 68 locomotive. Their new class of locos would find work on varied duties including scheduled and charter passenger trains, as well as their more familiar intermodal and nuclear flask freight traffic. This decision would ultimately lead to the withdrawal of some, if not all, of its older locomotive fleet.

Direct Rail Services had considered a number of potential manufacturers, including a possible order for General Electric's Class 70 locomotives, before turning to Swiss manufacturer, Stadler Rail. The result was the placement of an order for fifteen Class 68 locomotives, financed through Beacon Rail, for delivery from 2013 onwards. The UK design, given the name UKLight, was based on the EuroLight, which the manufacturer had already developed for the European market. The UK variant would have a higher maximum speed of 160 kilometres (100 miles) per hour and a larger fuel tank, with a capacity of 5,000 litres.

Once production had commenced, pioneer loco No. 68001 spent time at the Velim test track in the Czech Republic, meaning sister loco No. 68002 was the first to arrive in the United Kingdom in the spring of 2014.

The Class 68 locomotive's arrival heralded a new era in the business aspirations of Direct Rail Services. Each locomotive weighed 86 tons and was equipped with a 3,800 horsepower Caterpillar C175-16 power unit, a feature that soon earned the class the nickname 'Cats'. As already mentioned, these locos are owned by Beacon Rail and leased to Direct Rail Services (DRS). In turn, DRS have sub-leased a number of these locomotives to a variety of other passenger operating companies, as will be seen in more detail later.

Among the first passenger duties performed by the new Class 68s were the Chiltern Mainline services between London Marylebone and Birmingham's Moor Street and Snow Hill stations and, onwards, to Kidderminster. They were to replace the Class 67 locomotives, hired from DB Cargo, on these services commencing at the end of 2014. A batch of eight these Class 68 locos, Nos 68008 to 68015 inclusive, was equipped with the necessary AAR (Association of American Railroads) equipment to enable the push-pull operation of the services incorporating a driver vehicle trailer. Six of these Class 68 locos, Nos 68010 to 68015 inclusive, were also painted in Chiltern's silver main line livery.

Shortly afterwards, the passenger operator of Scottish Railways, Scotrail, also commenced using the class on two of its peak hour Fife Circle diagrams linking that county's commuter stations with Edinburgh's Haymarket and Waverley stations. Once again, Direct Rail Services obliged by outshopping two of its locos in Scotrail's saltire livery. The first of these peak hour commuter services between Edinburgh and Glenrothes commenced in April 2015, with the services continuing to run for more than five years. They ceased in May 2020.

Direct Rail Services has also provided its Class 68 locomotives to several other operators around the UK, notably along the Cumbrian Coast to supplement Northern Rail's diesel units and, likewise, assisting Greater Anglia to cover for diesel unit shortages on Suffolk and Norfolk secondary services to and from Norwich.

The company orders for its Class 68 locomotives were increased in stages to give a present fleet size of thirty-four locomotives. This increased fleet size was due in no small part to the provision of a dedicated pool of locos for passenger operator First TransPennine Express (FTPE). FTPE were allocated locomotives, numbered 68019 to 68032 inclusive, to haul new Mark 5A coaching stock on their core services across the Pennines. Initially, they were to see service on the Liverpool Lime Street to Scarborough route.

Loco No. 68021 was selected to visit the Velim Test Track in the Czech Republic for testing to work alongside FTPE's new fleet of Mark 5A coaches. The first Class 68-hauled passenger trains on the Liverpool to Scarborough route, via Manchester, Leeds and York, commenced in the summer of 2019, with a commitment that loco haulage on the route from Manchester to Redcar Central was to follow.

At the time of writing, it is believed the First Group is looking for an early termination of its franchise, which may have a bearing on the future of these locomotive-hauled services across the Pennines. In any event, a restricted timetable was in operation during the Covid-19 pandemic, with most loco-hauled operation restricted to the route between York and Scarborough.

Alongside the Class 68 loco fleet expansion, DRS also explored the concept of a 'dual-mode' locomotive capable of operating both from a diesel engine and via the electricity supply of overhead lines (OHLE). The result was the placement of an order for ten Class 88 locomotives that would closely resemble the Class 68 diesels in appearance. Furthermore, the majority of the locomotive components, about 70 per cent in total, would be shared between the two classes.

The locos, numbered 88001 to 88010 inclusive, were delivered to the UK during 2016 and 2017. The class has become the preferred choice of power for DRS's Anglo-Scottish intermodal services linking Daventry International Railfreight Terminal (DIRFT) in Northamptonshire with Mossend in Central Scotland. This route has overhead line equipment in place throughout, with the diesel power usually only being used at either end of the operation for any shunting required within the terminals, where there are no such overhead wires in place. The same end-to-end benefits of using Class 88 locomotives apply to the recently won contract to move Ford cars between their factory at Dagenham and Garston on Merseyside.

In this publication, we look closely at each member of the fleet of forty-four locos representing both classes. This is followed by a chapter on the depots at Carlisle and Crewe that service this DRS fleet. In particular, I would like to express my appreciation to the company's staff, notably at the depot open days. Their knowledge has made a valuable contribution to this book.

In addition to DRS's own workings in the nuclear and intermodal marketplace, we look at the service they provide to Network Rail as well as the other private operators outlined above.

We end with a miscellany of other workings around the country for these two classes of locomotive, often as a light engine or engines moving between their home depots and DRS's customers in order to carry out their revenue-earning duties.

# Class 68 Locomotives – No. 68001 to No. 68034 Inclusive

The Class 68 diesel locomotives first appeared in the United Kingdom in 2014. The first numbered, No. 68001 *Revolution,* spent some time on the test track at Velim in the Czech Republic, before arriving in this country later that year. It is seen here at Direct Rail Services' (DRS) depot at Gresty Bridge, in Crewe, on 12 June 2018.

The second locomotive numerically, No. 68002 *Intrepid*, was therefore the first of the class to arrive in the UK from Valencia, in Spain, earlier in that year. It is seen here three years after delivery, on 20 July 2017, stabled in the sidings adjacent to the Greater Anglia station at Norwich.

An initial order, financed through Beacon Rail, saw DRS take delivery of fifteen locos during 2014. The next in the numerical sequence was No. 68003 *Astute*. It is seen passing through Leicester station on 19 October 2016.

The fourth Class 68 locomotive member is No. 68004 *Rapid*. It is seen approaching Nuneaton on 18 June 2018. It is leading a convoy of locomotives heading light engines from Norwich to DRS's depot at Crewe Gresty Bridge.

The fifth loco, No. 68005 *Defiant,* was just under a year old when it is seen pausing in Leicester station on 25 March 2015.

The first five class members numerically have all retained their Direct Rail Services compass-style livery, as seen on the bodyside of No. 68005 in October 2017. In May 2021, DRS announced a further rebranding in line with that of its new parent company, Nuclear Transport Solutions (NTS). It is likely that the loco fleet will reflect this new branding in due course.

No. 68006 *Daring* was one of two locos chosen to carry Scotrail's saltire livery. This was in recognition of DRS's operation of two of the Scottish operator's commuter services between Edinburgh and Glenrothes between 2015 and 2020. The loco is seen waiting to leave Haymarket, in Edinburgh, on one of the evening peak services on 1 April 2015.

This 2015 cabside view of No. 68006 shows clearly why the livery has earned the nickname 'spotrail' among Scottish rail enthusiasts.

No. 68007 *Valiant* was the second loco chosen to have this Scotrail livery applied. The loco is just a few months old when seen here on 8 January 2015. This photo was taken shortly before the saltire livery was applied. It was seen at Nuneaton on a driver training run from Crewe.

Class 68 No.68008 *Avenger* was the first of the class numerically to be fitted with Association of American Railroads (AAR) push-pull equipment to enable them to work with Chiltern Railways' coaching stock and driving van trailer (DVT). An example of the Chiltern Railways' DVT appears later in this book. The loco is seen in the platform at Stourbridge Junction station on 8 May 2015.

Sister loco No. 68009 *Titan* was also fitted with the push-pull equipment for use on Chiltern Railways' services. On 2 August 2019, the locomotive is stabled in the West Yard, adjacent to Doncaster station.

Chiltern Railways livery was applied to six of the class members, with No. 68010 the first numerically. It is seen in London's Marylebone station on 29 June 2015. These six locos remained unnamed until No. 68010 was named *Oxford Flyer* in December 2016, recognising Chiltern's link with the city. To date this is the only one of the Chiltern Railways locomotives to be named.

The second Chiltern-liveried machine is No. 68011. It is seen awaiting departure from Leamington Spa station on 9 May 2018 on a service to Birmingham Moor Street.

The next loco to receive Chiltern Railways' main line livery was No. 68012. On 21 February 2017 it is seen being dragged by English Electric Type 3 No. 37422 through Derby station en route to Barrow Hill, Chesterfield.

On 5 September 2020, a Saturday, No. 68013 was photographed passing through Cheddington on the West Coast Main Line. It is heading for DRS's depot at Crewe. Saturday is generally the change over day for swapping the Chiltern Class 68s for any servicing required.

On 31 July 2018, No. 68014 is seen taking a break from its more usual Chiltern Railway duties. It is seen heading a Network Rail infrastructure working through Leicester.

The final Chiltern Railway-branded class member is No. 68015. This locomotive side view clearly shows the two-tone silver and grey livery applied to this batch of locos dedicated to this passenger operator. The photo was taken at Tyseley, West Midlands, on 24 April 2019.

The initial DRS order for fifteen locos was quickly followed by the placement of a second order of a further ten Class 68 locomotives. Delivery of this second batch, numbered from No. 68016 to No. 68025, commenced with No. 68016 *Fearless*. It is seen passing Tamworth (Low Level) on 30 March 2017.

The second loco in this batch was No. 68017 *Hornet*. It is seen on 7 June 2016 passing Nuneaton heading towards East Anglia. It has the company of a Greater Anglia Class 90 on this light engine move to Norwich.

The third loco in the batch was No. 68018 *Vigilant*. It is seen on 25 April 2019 at Leicester. These first three locos retain their DRS blue and green colours with the white compass logo.

Loco No. 68019 *Brutus* is the first of the sub pool of locos dedicated to First TransPennine (FTPE) services. It is seen on 4 February 2016, prior to being re-liveried in FTPE's house colours.

In this view, the next example, No. 68020 *Reliance,* is also seen prior to receiving FTPE colours. It was to be found in the headshunt at Mountsorrel Quarry, Leicestershire, on 4 July 2016. It has just stabled having uncoupled from its rake of empty wagons brought from Crewe for loading.

The 'TransPennine Express' branding had been applied to the bodyside of No. 68020 by the time this photo was taken at Scarborough in 2021.

The Class 68 loco details are carried on the cab door of No. 68020. This confirms, among other information, that the loco's weight is 85 tons and it has a maximum speed limit of 100 miles per hour. In common with their Class 88 sisters, the Class 68 route availability is RA7. This is at the upper end of the spectrum, but on a par with, for example, both the Class 66 and Class 70 locomotives.

By the time this photo was taken at Stafford on 9 March 2018, No. 68021 *Tireless* had received FTPE livery. This loco, together with No. 68019, was chosen to move to the test track at Velim, in the Czech Republic, to be evaluated alongside the Mark 5A coaching stock. The first attempt to deliver the locos via Dollands Moor and the Channel Tunnel proved unsuccessful and they were returning to Crewe. After another unsuccessful move, which got as far as Calais before returning home, they were then routed via the port of Immingham and Cuxenhaven, Germany, to reach Velim at the third attempt.

Class 68 No. 68022 *Resolution,* together with sister loco No. 68021, were the next arrivals at the Port of Workington from Valencia, in Spain. The pair was transferred from the dockside at Workington to DRS's depot at Carlisle Kingmoor in March 2016. In July the same year, No. 68022 is seen arriving at Derby on a light engine move from Crewe.

A month later in April 2016, a further trio of new locos, No. 68023 to No. 68025, were the next to arrive from Spain and moved from Workington Docks to Carlisle Kingmoor. No. 68023 *Achilles* is seen just a few weeks later, on 23 June, pausing at Bletchley on a coaching stock move to Wembley.

The second locomotive of that trio, No. 68024 *Centaur*, is seen at Leicester on 21 March 2017. The three locos were delivered in plain blue colours with the DRS blue and green vinyls subsequently applied at Carlisle's Kingmoor depot.

No. 68025 *Superb* completed the second batch of deliveries and had received the FTPE livery when photographed at Nuneaton on 1 July 2019. The loco and stock were involved in mileage accumulation ahead of their entry into service across the Pennines.

A third order of seven locomotives, No. 68026 to No. 68032 inclusive, was to follow with completion of delivery to the UK in summer 2017. The first of these, No. 68026 *Enterprise,* is seen on 25 March 2019, propelling a rake of FTPE stock.

No. 68027 *Splendid* also arrived at Workington Docks in March 2017. It is seen here on 7 January 2020 in First TransPennine Express colours.

The next four locos, No. 68028 to No. 68031, arrived in the UK two months later. They were moved from the docks at Workington to Carlisle, and then, a day or so later, to the DRS depot at Crewe Gresty Bridge. The first of these, No. 68028, later to be named *Lord President,* is seen here in early September that year while still in DRS's colours.

The second in the batch, No. 68029 *Courageous*, which had received its FTPE livery when stabled at York on 8 January 2020.

The third of these four locos, No. 68030 *Black Douglas*, is also seen at York. This photo was taken on 8 October 2019.

The final loco in this batch of deliveries in May 2017 was No. 68031 *Felix*. It is seen at Leicester on 24 April 2019.

By the time No. 68032 *Destroyer* arrived in the UK, DRS had already ordered a further two locos, No. 68033 and No. 68034. These three locos therefore arrived on the same vessel at Workington Docks in July 2017. Loco No. 68032 is seen here at York on 8 October 2019.

Loco No. 68033 was the first of two additional locos ordered, chiefly, to provide cover for the First TransPennine pool of No. 68019 to No. 68032 inclusive. This loco retains its original DRS livery and, to date, remains unnamed. It is seen at its Carlisle base in July 2019.

The final class member, No. 68034, also retains its DRS colours and it, too, is currently unnamed. It is seen at Nuneaton just a few weeks after it had been delivered.

## Class 88 Locomotives – No. 88001 to No. 88010 Inclusive

During the course of delivery of the Class 68 diesel locomotives, a dual-mode variant was proposed by Stadler. This could be powered either by use of the loco's diesel engine or, alternatively, via overhead electric power supply. The first of the class numerically, No. 88001 *Revolution* is seen at Nuneaton on 19 November 2018.

With No. 88001 under test at the Velim test track in the Czech Republic, No. 88002 *Prometheus* became the first of the Class 88 locos to be delivered to the United Kingdom, arriving in January 2017. No. 88002 is seen here passing through Crewe station on 29 August 2019.

All ten members of the class had been delivered by March 2017, including No. 88003 *Genesis*. It is seen at Direct Rail Services's Carlisle Kingmoor depot in October that year.

The next class member is No. 88004 *Pandora*. Unlike their Class 68 counterparts, all members of the class, including No. 88004, carry DRS's own branding. The loco is seen in Doncaster's West Yard on 29 January 2019.

Loco No. 88005 carries the name *Minerva*. As this photo, taken at Tamworth on 29 August 2019, shows, with the obvious exception of the pantograph connection to the OHLE, the external appearance of the two classes is virtually identical.

Loco No. 88006 *Juno* arrived in the UK at the end of March 2017, in the company of No. 88007, No. 88009, No. 88010 and a pair of Class 68s. It is seen standing in Doncaster's West Yard on 7 June 2018.

Sister loco, No. 88007 *Electra,* which arrived in the same shipment from Spain in March 2017, is seen leading a light engine convoy through Nuneaton on 17 September 2017.

No. 88008 *Ariadne* was the fifth loco, along with No. 88001, No. 88003, No. 88004 and No. 88005, to arrive in Workington Docks at the beginning of March 2017 aboard the ship *Eemslift Nelli*. No. 88008 is seen heading north through Doncaster station on 6 September 2018.

The penultimate member of the class is No. 88009 *Diana*. It is seen at work heading north at Oubeck, near Lancaster, on 2 October 2017.

The final member of the class is No. 88010 *Aurora*, seen here at Floriston, north of Carlisle, on 20 July 2019.

The arrival of the Class 68 locomotives marked a significant step forward in DRS's choice of motive power. It was highly appropriate, therefore, that first-numbered class member, No. 68001, arrived in the UK sporting the name *Evolution*.

Three years later, No. 88001 was to carry a similarly appropriate nameplate: *Revolution*, not least because it was the pioneer dual-mode locomotive in the UK.

The first nine Class 68 locomotives, No. 68001 to No. 68009, arrived in the UK already carrying their respective nameplates. No. 68008, for example, is named *Avenger*, a name once carried by 1960s diesel loco D804, a Warship class locomotive.

Most of the thirty-four Class 68s have subsequently been named, with the exception of No. 68011 to No. 68015 (Chiltern) and the final two examples, No. 68033 and No. 68034. It is surely more than a coincidence that No. 68030 was chosen to carry the name *Black Douglas*, a name once carried by West Coast Main Line electric loco No. 87030 some forty years earlier.

The ten Class 88 locos are all named, with No. 88002 *Prometheus* carrying the same name once carried by Class 76 electric locomotive E26055, later to become No. 76055.

Seven of the ten Class 88 locomotives were to receive the same names as the seven Class 77 locomotives that once operated the now closed Woodhead route between Manchester and Sheffield. These seven namings include No. 88010 *Aurora*, a name once carried by E27002 until it was scrapped in the mid-1980s.

In addition to their nameplates, all locos prominently display their works plates fitted by either Vossloh or Stadler prior to delivery. Locos No. 68001 to No. 68025 carry Vossloh numbers 2679 to 2703 inclusive, including No. 68023 *Achilles,* which carries Vossloh No. 2701, dating from 2015.

Likewise, the Stadler-manufactured members of both classes carry that company's works plates. The ten Class 88 locos carry Stadler works numbers 2851 to 2860 inclusive. The remaining Class 68 locos carry Stadler 2944 to 2950 on locos No. 68026 to No. 68032, with No. 68033 and No. 68034 numbered 3038 and 3039 respectively. The Stadler works plate number 2947, dating from 2017, is shown here on No. 68029 *Courageous.*

# Direct Rail Services Locomotive Depots at Carlisle and Crewe

The Direct Rail Services depots at Carlisle and Crewe, together with the Cumbrian town of Sellafield, are the homes of the Class 68 and Class 88 locomotives. This impressive banner greeted visitors to the open day at the company's Kingmoor depot in Carlisle in July 2019.

This view of the south end of the Carlisle depot area shows examples of the company's veteran Class 37 diesel locos, numbered No. 37419 *Carl Haviland 1954–2012* and No. 37409 *Lord Hinton*, alongside No. 68022 *Resolution*.

Unnamed No. 68033 was another one of the locos on display at the north end of Carlisle Kingmoor depot complex at the same depot open day in July 2019, offering visitors a chance to take a close look at the locos.

An immaculate dual-mode Class 88 loco, No. 88009 *Diana*, is proudly displayed inside Carlisle's Kingmoor depot having spent several days on the depot prior to the event.

Class 68 No. 68017 was also on display inside the depot on 20 July 2019. It had worked along the Cumbrian coast from DRS's Sellafield base a couple of days earlier prior to going on show at the depot.

This Class 68 is named *Hornet*. It was an appropriate choice for open day visitors to see first-hand the interior of the loco, offering a glimpse inside the 'hornet's nest'.

This is the inside view of the cab controls of the Class 68 loco, operation of which was willingly explained by the depot staff on hand at the open day.

This is the view from the number 1 cab of No. 68017. It gives an insight to the driver's view. In this case, that view is of the other locos on display inside the depot that day.

This view shows No. 68017 *Hornet* in the centre, with No. 68018 *Vigilant* on the left. Two of the company's older machines, Nos 66424 and 57303 are on the right.

This close-up of No. 68018 *Vigilant* shows the loco on display at the entrance to Kingmoor depot during the open day. The loco had arrived back in Carlisle having earlier worked a nuclear flask train to and from Hunterston in Scotland.

On Monday 2 October 2017, it is business as usual at the depot. This is the familiar view on the approach road to Carlisle Kingmoor depot entrance. The line up on the right consists of No. 88004 *Pandora*, No. 88005 *Minerva*, No. 57302, No. 88006 *Juno* and No. 57305. The West Coast Main Line is immediately behind the fence on the right.

The depot's prime position adjacent to the West Coast Main Line makes for an easy crew change on Anglo-Scottish freight workings. On 9 October 2018, for example, No. 88001 *Revolution* is seen waiting for its driver to take this southbound intermodal forward. The depot complex is to the left of the loco, behind the fence. The depot had been in disuse since 1987 until Direct Rail Services moved into the Kingmoor site in 1998.

The weather was far less kind at the DRS open day at Crewe Gresty Bridge depot on 19 July 2014. With the many enthusiasts struggling with the persistent rain, No. 68002 *Intrepid* is displayed outside the depot doors, with sister No. 68001 *Evolution* on the left.

Back inside the comfort of the depot, No. 68006 *Daring* offers open day visitors what will be, for many, their first close-up look inside the cab of a Class 68 loco.

Sister loco No. 68007 *Valiant* was also on display inside the depot that day, with the many visitors pleased to get out of the rain and enjoy a close-up look at this impressive loco.

Pioneer No. 68001 *Evolution* was again present on the Crewe depot on 12 June 2018. At the time, the loco had just returned from a period working in East Anglia.

This view shows the old and the new at Crewe Gresty Bridge on 7 April 2019. Almost fifty years separate the building of the veteran English Electric Type 3, numbered 37402, in 1965 and both No. 68016 *Fearless* and No. 88004 *Pandora,* built in the mid-2010s.

The same day, No. 68027 *Splendid* is visible from the approach road to the depot entrance. This loco had been moving between here and Longsight, in Manchester, in readiness for First TransPennine Express working.

## Nuclear Flask Traffic

Since 1995, Nuclear Fuel trains have been exclusively handled by Direct Rail Services, linking a number of UK sites with its BNFL Sellafield base. These services were handled by its fleet of older locos for approximately twenty years before gradual replacement by Class 68 and Class 88 locos. On 28 June 2017, No. 68001 *Evolution* heads a single flask carrier north through Stafford.

A pair of locos is always used on these nuclear flask workings and on this occasion the second loco is No. 68030, since named *Black Douglas*. The pair are heading from Bridgwater to Crewe, where they will stable before later working northwards to their base at Sellafield.

The Welsh nuclear power station at Wylfa, on the island of Anglesey, was switched off at the end of 2015 after half a century of use. The nearby rail sidings at Valley offer a convenient loading point for the used nuclear fuel elements rail journey eastwards to Crewe and then onward to Sellafield. On 13 June 2018, No. 68018 *Vigilant* leads No. 68002 *Intrepid* through Llanfair PG with a pair of flask carriers.

This rear view of the working shows the two FNA irradiated fuel flask wagons, numbers 550054 and 550059, which were built in the 1980s. They have since been displaced by a pool of newly built replacements.

Nuclear flask traffic also moves to Sellafield from the nuclear power station at Hunterston, in North Ayrshire, Scotland. On 19 July 2019, No. 68003 *Astute* heads through Carlisle station with a working from Hunterston back to its Sellafield base.

These flask workings are now regularly hauled by a paired combination of one Class 68 and one Class 88 locomotive. On the above working, the second engine in this pairing is No. 88002 *Prometheus* and the two more modern FNA wagons, which were built two years ago, are numbered 7092290255 and 7092290362. The train will now take the Cumbrian Coast line to reach its destination.

# Network Rail Infrastructure Traffic

Since rail privatisation, workings in connection with maintenance of the rail network have been split across the major freight operators, including Direct Rail Services. On 24 April 2019, No. 68031 *Felix* heads north through Leicester with a rake of box wagons from Crewe's Basford Hall Yard for loading at the nearby quarry at Mountsorrel.

On 9 March 2018, it was the turn of No. 68004 *Rapid* to be selected for this inbound working. It is seen crawling through Leicester's station platform waiting for the signal to proceed north. Locomotive haulage of this long standing, daily DRS working between Crewe and Mountsorrel is generally split between their Class 66 and Class 68 locomotives.

Once loaded, the return working heads northwards from Mountsorrel to regain the West Coast Main Line (WCML) at Lichfield Trent Valley. On 27 May 2016, No. 68001 *Evolution* passes Loughborough shortly after leaving the quarry with its loaded rake.

When not employed on their allocated Chiltern Railway duties, Chiltern-liveried locos from this pool occasionally appear on this Network Rail working. On 23 May 2016, for example, No. 68012 made an appearance and is seen here heading through Burton on Trent. At Wichnor Junction it will take the short, freight-only spur to Lichfield Trent Valley and then north on the WCML to Crewe.

On 8 June 2016, this northbound loaded working had already reached the West Coast Main Line. No. 68003 *Astute* appears out of the mist as it approaches Stafford on the return journey to Crewe Basford Hall Yard.

The Leicestershire quarry at Mountsorrel also provides stone for Network Rail's infrastructure base at Carlisle, as and when required. Class 68 locomotives often provide the power for this working also. On 3 May 2017, No. 68027 hauls the loaded working on the southern approach to Chesterfield, returning to Carlisle.

Another regular DRS infrastructure working links the rail yards at Basford Hall in Crewe, firstly with Bescot, near Birmingham, and then to Toton, on the Derbyshire and Nottinghamshire border. Again, their Class 68 locos are frequently used on this service. On 30 March 2017, No. 68021 *Tireless* has just arrived in Bescot Yard from Crewe.

On 21 July 2020, FTPE-liveried No. 68023 *Achilles* has just commenced the second leg of its journey from Crewe to Toton. It Is seen passing through Water Orton, on the outskirts of Birmingham, with a rake of 'JNA' box wagons.

On the East Coast Main Line on 26 January 2017, No. 68021 *Tireless* has just left Doncaster's yards and is heading north through the station. It is on a short trip working to York's Thrall yards.

A much longer trip was ahead of No. 88008 *Ariadne* on 6 September 2018. At that time, Direct Rail Services handled the infrastructure workings between Doncaster and Edinburgh's Millerhill Yard. It is seen passing northward through Doncaster's platform with a mixed rake of wagons. This service is at present in the hands of Colas Rail.

The Class 68 locomotives also made appearances on the Network Rail test trains to and from the Network Rail base at Derby. On 16 September 2016, No. 68021 *Tireless* heads into Derby on a return working from Old Oak Common, West London.

The Network Rail test train will reverse in the platform at Derby, leaving sister loco No. 68005 *Defiant* to lead on the short run round the curve to the depot at nearby Litchurch Lane.

# Intermodal Traffic

Since 2002, DRS have operated intermodal freight trains in the UK, initially between Grangemouth in Central Scotland and the International Rail Freight Terminal at Daventry, in Northamptonshire. Typically, two containers are carried on each twin wagon, an example of which is No. 6849091697, built in 1999 for this purpose and seen here on the rear of a northbound working from Daventry.

On 2 March 2020, this typical intermodal working is seen heading northbound through Nuneaton. The service is from Daventry to Mossend Yard, to the east of Glasgow. It is in the hands of No. 88001 *Evolution*.

These Anglo-Scottish services have recently been handled by Class 88 dual-mode locomotives. The fully electrified West Coast Main Line enables the locos to operate under electric power for virtually the entire route. On 1 July 2019, No. 88010 *Aurora* is in charge of the lunchtime northbound service from Daventry, seen passing through Nuneaton.

A month or so later, on 15 August 2019, it is the turn of No. 88008 *Ariadne* to haul the same Daventry to Mossend service. It will cover a distance of just over 300 miles, an alternative to around seventy lorry journeys covering a similar distance by road.

Heading in the opposite direction on 16 August 2019, No. 88007 *Electra* is afforded the privilege of running on the Up (southbound) main line as it passes Nuneaton on its journey to Daventry International Rail Freight Terminal.

It is more commonplace for these intermodal workings to use the slow lines while running on the four track section of WCML in the Trent Valley. On 27 August 2019, No. 88005 *Minerva* does just that as it heads south.

Russell Logistics have been major users of the rail network for almost half a century, working on behalf of supermarket and FMCG companies. Their services from Daventry to Scotland have been running for more than twenty years. On 16 January 2020, No. 88001 *Evolution* heads south through Tamworth's Low Level platforms.

On 5 March 2020, No. 88006 *Juno* heads through Tamworth Low Level in the opposite direction. These services take between seven and eight hours to complete the journey from Daventry to Mossend.

An earlier working left Daventry at around 06.30 in the morning and, about three hours later, is seen passing Oubeck Goods Loop on 2 October 2017. These loops are located a few miles south of Lancaster. The loco in charge that day is No. 88009 *Diana*.

The same loco, No. 88009 *Diana*, is in charge the following day when, an hour or so later in the day, the service is on the southern approach to Carlisle station.

On 19 July 2019, another working pauses briefly in the platform at Carlisle, with No. 88001 *Endeavour* at the helm. These trains usually operate fully loaded with sixteen twin wagons in each rake. On the northbound journeys the locomotives have to contend with the climbs at both Shap and Beattock.

With the climb over Shap summit, in the Lake District, already completed, another Class 88 readies itself for tackling Beattock, in the Scottish borders. On 20 July 2019, No. 88010 *Aurora* has just left Carlisle and approaches Floriston level crossing, close to the Scottish border.

These workings are routinely handled by single Class 88 locomotives for most, if not all, of their journey. Occasionally, a double-header is noted, such as on 26 November 2019. On that day, No. 88007 *Electra* and No. 88009 *Diana* were at the head of the southbound working to Daventry as they pass Nuneaton.

Class 68 locomotives are less common on these intermodals at present. On 15 January 2015, No. 68003 *Astute* was employed on a wagon move between Daventry and DRS's wagon repair depot at Motherwell. It is seen heading north through Nuneaton with a short rake of intermodal twin wagons.

# Chiltern Railways Main Line Services

This passenger operator runs services between London Marylebone and Birmingham's Moor Street and Snow Hill stations. Since 2014, Chiltern Railways have sub-leased Class 68 locomotives from DRS to operate some of these main line services. On 29 June 2015, No. 68010 waits to leave London Marylebone on a 13.15 service to Birmingham Moor Street.

The Class 68 diesel locomotive is normally positioned at the Birmingham, or 'country', end of the rake of coaching stock on these services, as was the case in this view of No. 68011 at London Marylebone on 24 September 2015.

These services operate with a Driving Van Trailer (DVT) at the London end of the rake of coaching stock. The Class 68 locos are fitted with the compatible AAR (Association of American Railroad) push-pull equipment. DVT No. 82302 is seen heading for London Marylebone through King's Sutton on 6 May 2021, with loco No. 68009 *Titan* providing the power and propelling on the rear.

Leamington Spa is one of the regular calling points on these main line services. On 9 May 2018, No. 68009 is seen leaving the Warwickshire station on the rear of the 13.20 service to London Marylebone, with the DVT already taking the curve.

Exactly a year earlier, No. 68014 is also seen pulling away from Leamington Spa. It is heading in the opposite direction on a service bound for Birmingham Moor Street.

Further north, No. 68008 *Avenger* waits in one of the terminus platforms at Birmingham's Moor Street station on 9 November 2015. It will shortly propel its train back to London Marylebone.

In recent years, considerable improvements have been carried out by both Chiltern Railways and Network Rail in an effort to make these services an attractive alternative to the competing Avanti Service using the West Coast Main Line. On 7 November 2017, No. 68013 speeds through King's Sutton on a Marylebone to Birmingham service that will take 105 minutes for the 111-mile journey. By comparison, Avanti services from London Euston to Birmingham New Street take approximately 80 minutes.

Some peak-hour services are further extended within the West Midlands to give Stourbridge Junction and Kidderminster a direct service to the capital. On 8 May 2015, No. 68008 is seen reversing past the signal box and sidings at Stourbridge Junction.

Servicing of Chiltern Railways' stock is undertaken at the company's traincare facility at Wembley Stadium. On 19 June 2015, the depot is home to No. 68012 when viewed from passing on the Chiltern running lines.

The Chiltern Traincare Facility at Aylesbury also sees occasional visits from Class 68 locomotives and coaching stock. On 17 October 2015, No. 68008 is seen jutting out of the depot entrance.

## Scotrail – Fife Circle Services

From April 2015, DRS Class 68 locomotives were hired by Scotrail to cover for their multiple unit fleet. These were employed on peak-hour services between Glenrothes, Fife, and Edinburgh. On the morning of 5 October 2017, No. 68005 *Defiant* was first to arrive at Haymarket on its inbound journey to Edinburgh Waverley.

Fifteen minutes later, No. 68006 *Daring* arrives at Haymarket on the second of the two morning locomotive-hauled peak services on the Fife Circle. It, too, will set down passengers here at Haymarket before making the short journey into Edinburgh Waverley.

Two, locomotive-hauled, evening peak services return around the Fife Circle for homebound commuters. On 1 April 2015, No. 68006 *Daring* is again in use on these services. This loco, together with sister No. 68007, were both outshopped in Scotrail livery in recognition of this partnership with the Scottish Rail operator.

The two Scotrail-liveried locos were often substituted with other class members on these workings. On 22 October 2018, for example, No. 68016 *Fearless* was employed on the second evening service.

Both these services were regularly formed of six Mark 2 coaches and continued in operation until early 2020 when the number of passengers fell sharply with the onset of the Covid-19 pandemic. On 24 October 2018, No. 68006 *Daring* hauls its six coaches into Haymarket station.

Servicing of the coaching stock was handled by the DRS depot at nearby Motherwell. On 16 October 2017, No. 68004 *Rapid* heads a rake of empty stock through Whifflet, in the Coatbridge suburbs.

# Greater Anglia – Norwich Branch Line Services

Direct Rail Services have also provided motive power cover for shortages of diesel multiple units on Greater Anglia's branches in Norfolk and Suffolk. Pairs of Class 68 locomotives worked alongside pairs of the older Class 37s until 2017. On 29 September 2016, No. 68024 *Centaur* and No. 37405 both stand in Norwich station.

The Class 68 locomotives worked in top-and-tail formation with a short three-coach rake between Norwich and the coastal towns of Lowestoft and Great Yarmouth. On this occasion, No. 68024 *Centaur* is joined by No. 68022 *Resolution* on the rear.

On 7 September 2017, the 14.05 service from Norwich to Lowestoft was in the hands of No. 68001 *Evolution* and No. 68028. The latter locomotive, unnamed at the time, leads the train as it leaves Reedham. The semaphore signals at this location were due to be replaced shortly after this photo was taken.

In this second view on departure from Reedham, No. 68001 *Evolution* brings up the rear of the train.

On 20 July 2017, No. 68005 *Defiant* is seen at the buffer stops at Lowestoft, having just arrived from Norwich. A veteran unit on a service to Ipswich stands in the adjacent platform. It was their increasing unreliability that led to these locomotive-hauled sets being provided as cover.

With a limited turnaround time at Lowestoft in order to maintain the usual unit timetable, No. 68024 *Centaur* will shortly depart leading the train on its return Greater Anglia working to Norwich.

The locos and coaches were not required by Greater Anglia for their originally booked services on 23 May 2017. No. 68003 *Astute* was therefore stabled out of use in the sidings adjacent to Norwich station.

On that day, it was partnered with No. 68022 *Resolution*, seen on the opposite end of the rake of coaches.

These Class 68 locomotive pairings also worked services from Norwich to Great Yarmouth. On 20 July 2017, No. 68005 *Defiant* is waiting at Norwich to form an afternoon service to the Norfolk resort. The regular use of these DRS locos was to cease a few weeks later.

Class 68 locomotive swaps between Norwich and their depot at Crewe were occasionally used to facilitate other stock moves. One such working on 29 September 2016 saw No. 68004 *Rapid* collect Greater Anglia's DVT numbered 82112 en route. The pair are seen passing through Ipswich station on the Great Eastern Main Line.

# Northern on the Cumbrian Coast and Furness Line

DRS's Class 68 locomotives found themselves giving a helping hand much closer to home in 2018, providing more modern motive power to assist Northern with their service along the Cumbrian Coast. No. 68017 *Hornet* calls at the small Cumbrian village of Foxfield working the 06.16 service from Carlisle to Barrow-in-Furness.

The pair of Class 68s was provided to replace the veteran class 37s, which were suffering from poor reliability issues at a time when Northern's overall failing performance was under the spotlight. Operating in top-and-tail mode, No. 68003 *Astute* is on the rear of the service as it leaves Foxfield.

The same combination was seen on the return service from Barrow at 09.18. No. 68003 is now seen leading the Northern service as it arrives at Millom.

The Northern service is about to depart Millom with No. 68017 on the rear. The three-coach rake includes DRS's former driving brake standard open, numbered 9705 next to the rear locomotive.

# First TransPennine Express services (FTPE)

The much-heralded return of loco-hauled trains across the Pennines led to FTPE leasing a number of Class 68 locomotives from DRS. Prior to entry into revenue-earning passenger service, the chosen rolling stock was required to undergo mileage accumulation on the West Coast Main Line. On 1 July 2019, No. 68025 *Superb* propels a rake of FTPE stock south through Nuneaton.

These trains consist of a five-coach set of mark 5A coaches, with a driving trailer at the opposite end to the locomotive. On 18 February 2020, No. 68030 *Black Douglas* is seen at Tamworth Low Level propelling FTPE set TP08 on a run from Carlisle to Bletchley.

With the FTPE Mark 5A coach sets based at Alstom's Manchester Longsight depot, their diagram usually involved a run from Manchester to Carlisle, then south on the WCML to Bletchley, or Rugby before returning north to Manchester. On 17 June 2017, No. 68031 *Felix* takes a turn on this diagram, and is seen speeding south through Nuneaton.

As mentioned, each of these FTPE coach sets has a Driving Trailer (DT) built by CAF in Northern Spain. These DTs avoid the need for locos to run round their stock at termini or double-up locomotives because they operate in push-pull formation. On 28 August 2018, DT numbered 12802 leads FT set TP02, and locomotive No. 68020 *Reliance* brings up the rear. The train is returning north from Rugby to Alstom's depot at Longsight, Manchester.

Fourteen Class 68 locomotives, numbered No. 68019 to No. 68032 inclusive, were initially earmarked for these FTPE services. Later, No. 68033 and No. 68034 were added to the pool in order to give additional cover. On 8 October 2019, No. 68020 *Reliance* is seen heading through York station on a driver training run.

The fourteen dedicated locomotives were each given the FTPE livery, as seen here on No. 68032 *Destroyer*, which was stabled in the parcel sidings adjacent to York station on the same day.

These locos and coaching stock sets were initially to be employed on services between Liverpool Lime Street and Scarborough, with the route between Manchester and Redcar Central to be added later. On 8 October 2019, No. 68030 *Black Douglas* awaits departure from under York station's overall roof while working a Liverpool to Scarborough service.

No. 68027 *Splendid* is seen working in the opposite direction as it passes Colton Junction and heads for its next stop at Garforth, on the eastern edge of Leeds, on 7 January 2020 on a Scarborough to Liverpool Lime Street service. When the FTPE timetable is in full operation, the junction at Colton offers a good vantage point to view these services.

At the eastern terminus for this route, both No. 68020 *Reliance* and No. 68021 *Tireless* rest at the buffers at Scarborough station. In this view, on 8 January 2020, No. 68021 has just terminated on a service from Liverpool Lime Street.

This view from the buffers shows No. 68020 on the left and sister No. 68021 on the right in Scarborough station. With a full timetable, and driver training in operation, a total of four members of the class were at this seaside resort in a two-hour period that morning.

At the opposite end of Scarborough station, No. 68023 *Achilles* waits to form the next FTPE service to Liverpool Lime Street. These services are scheduled to cover the end-to-end journey of just over 140 miles in just under three hours.

The turnaround at Scarborough enables a glimpse of the interior of one of the Mark 5A coaches on these services. It is a Trailer Standard coach, numbered 12712. These coaches were built by CAF and delivery to the UK commenced in 2019.

These TransPennine services have only a minute or two dwell time on average at each of their stops en route. Just four minutes was allowed at York for this service, as No. 68023 calls three quarters of an hour after leaving Scarborough.

This view of No. 68029 *Courageous* in the former Scarborough bay platform at York was taken on 8 October 2019. It had just returned from a driver training run earlier that day.

On 10 September 2019, No. 68026 *Enterprise* approaches Leeds on a service to Scarborough. Sadly, loco-hauled journeys such as this one to the west of York, onward to Manchester and Liverpool, were curtailed during the period of the Covid-19 emergency timetable. Only one early morning through working from Liverpool to Scarborough was loco-hauled in this period. These Class 68 workings were, therefore, mostly confined to the North Yorkshire stretch between York and Scarborough.

No. 68020 *Reliance* is seen propelling an eastbound service on 25 May 2021. This TransPennine service is a curtailed one operating between York and Scarborough only. During a torrential downpour, the train is seen passing Weaverthorpe level crossing, between Malton and Seamer.

Earlier that day, the same loco waited at Scarborough while forming one of the hourly services to Seamer, Malton and York only. FTPE's unit No. 185103 stands in the platform on the left.

Driving trailer No. 12804 leads another Scarborough to York service as it enters the single platform at Malton station on 25 May 2021.

No. 68026 *Enterprise* is on the rear of the train, propelling the service with TPE set 04 towards York. It is seen as it departs Malton station.

With DRS Class 66s, including No. 66424, for company, No. 68029 stands adjacent to York station on 8 January 2020. With First TransPennine Express looking for an early termination of their franchise, it brings into question the future of these fourteen Class 68 locomotives and their dedicated livery.

# A Miscellany of Other Class 68 and Class 88 Workings

The first passenger workings for a Direct Rail Services Class 88 locomotive occurred on 9 May 2017. No. 88002 *Prometheus* hauled a charter from London Euston to Carlisle. The train is seen arriving at Milton Keynes Central.

No. 68022 *Resolution* was on the rear of this working. It was a Northern Belle DRS charter packaged as 'The Class 88 VIP Launch Train'. The charter train was organised as a joint venture between Direct Rail Services and specialist charter operator Hertfordshire Rail Tours.

A year earlier, on 23 June 2016, No. 68023 *Achilles* is seen at Bletchley on another passenger working, this time for the Branch Line Society. This working was the annual fundraising 'Three Peaks Challenge' for the Railway Children charity. No. 57301 was on the opposite end of the train.

Chiltern-liveried No. 68012 was used for a more mundane working on 5 June 2015. It was called upon to collect a single twin flat wagon, numbered 7049010705, from W. H. Davis's wagon works at Shirebrook, and take it to Derby.

The provision of motive power for services operated for Network Rail often involves light engine moves between DRS's Crewe Gresty Bridge depot and the Network Rail base at Derby. On 5 February 2019, No. 68003 *Astute* leads one such Class 68 pairing into Derby station.

After reversal, sister Class 68 loco No. 68005 *Defiant* will then head towards Derby Litchurch Lane to enable the pair to commence a few days working with the Network Rail Test Train.

Derby station is again the location of this light engine move involving DRS's No. 37423 dragging No. 68001 *Evolution* north through the platform. The veteran English Electric Type 3 was taking an almost brand new Class 68 locomotive from Crewe Gresty Bridge to Barrow Hill, near Chesterfield.

A few raised eyebrows from the gathered enthusiasts accompanied the sighting of Scotrail-liveried No. 68006 *Daring* at Derby on 2 February 2016. More likely to be found working in Central Scotland, the loco had just arrived on a light engine move from Crewe and was to spend a few days on examination here before returning to its Gresty Bridge base.

DRS has recently secured a contract to move cars from Dagenham, in Essex, to Garston on Merseyside. This has brought a welcome variation to the sight of Class 88 locomotives on the West Coast Main Line (WCML). On 20 May 2021, No. 88009 *Diana* is seen as it exits Linslade Tunnel, just to the north of Leighton Buzzard.

A few miles further south on the WCML, on 1 February 2020, No. 68012 is seen passing Cheddington accompanied by No. 37401 *Mary Queen of Scots*. The pair are working from Willesden northwards to the DRS depot at Crewe Gresty Bridge.

A similar move on 31 January 2017 saw a pair of Class 68 locomotives heading north through Bletchley station. No. 68025 *Superb* leads No. 68005 *Defiant* on an overcast winter's day.

Another light engine move in connection with Chiltern Railways, on 20 March 2015, saw their liveried No. 68014 pass through Smethwick Galton Bridge in the West Midlands. It was working from their traincare depot at Wembley Stadium.

While the class were being introduced on Daventry intermodal workings, Class 88 locomotives frequently stabled just a few miles away at the south end of Rugby station. On 19 June 2017, No. 88003 *Genesis* is seen stabled there alongside a pair of much older machines, No. 57307 *Thunderbirds – Lady Penelope* and No. 86259 *Peter Pan*.

In order to change the locomotives on their Anglo-Scottish intermodal workings to and from Daventry, DRS frequently move locos between the Northamptonshire Rail Freight Terminal and their Crewe Gresty Bridge depot. On 19 November 2018, for example, No. 88001 *Revolution* is seen heading north through Nuneaton on a light engine move back to Crewe.

A more unusual Class 88 locomotive light engine move through Nuneaton occurred on 26 November 2018. No. 88005 *Minerva* is making use of its diesel engine, at least for the non-electrified part of its journey. It was working from Stud Farm quarry in Leicestershire back to DRS's depot at Crewe.

Not long after arrival in the UK, this pair of Class 68s, No. 68019 *Brutus* and No. 68018 *Vigilant*, are seen at Crewe on 4 February 2016 on a move from their Carlisle Kingmoor depot. They are heading to Electro-Motive Diesel Ltd's maintenance centre at Longport, Stoke on Trent.

Another class member is seen at Crewe station on 22 September 2017. No. 68031, unnamed at the time but later named *Felix*, is seen reversing in the Shrewsbury bay platform ready to make the short trip back to the local depot at Gresty Bridge.

For many years, Greater Anglia's Class 90 electric locomotives visited Crewe for attention. They were often taken back to their Norwich Crown Point depot via a DRS Class 68 locomotive move. On 7 June 2016, No. 68017 *Hornet* hauls No. 90008 *The East Anglian* south through Nuneaton. It will be routed via Willesden, the London suburbs and the Great Eastern Main Line to reach Norwich.

Direct Rail Services' light engine moves between Norwich Crown Point and Crewe are often routed cross-country via Peterborough, rather than via London. On 23 January 2017, No. 68017 *Hornet* leads No. 37422 through Nuneaton as the pair head back to their Gresty Bridge depot.

On 18 June 2018, no fewer than four Class 68 locomotives, together with No. 37419 *Carl Haviland 1954–2012*, were involved in a similar move from Norwich to Crewe when seen through Nuneaton. With No. 68004 *Rapid* leading, the convoy also included No. 68001 *Evolution*, No. 68018 *Vigilant* and No. 68002 *Intrepid*.

On 9 September 2014, a pair of Class 68s were involved in another light engine move involving Greater Anglia's Norwich Crown Point depot. No. 68011 and No. 68009 *Titan* are seen heading north through Peterborough, destined for York Thrall Works. They were to return to Stowmarket the next day with a rake of wagons for that autumn's rail head treatment trains.

The first and last members of Class 68 were captured in this light engine move through Nuneaton on 18 September 2017. With No. 37405 sandwiched between them, No. 68034, unnamed at the time, leads No. 68001 *Evolution* on a Willesden to Crewe light engine working.

An even more spectacular convoy was seen through Tamworth Low Level on 4 February 2015. DRS's Nos 66302 and 57312 are at the front of this five loco move. The three locos on the rear are all Chiltern Class 68s. No. 68013, nearest the camera, is seen on the very rear with No. 68011 and No. 68010. The impressive quintet is working from Willesden to Crewe.